Viktor Orbán's War on Migration

Hungary's Battle for Sovereignty and the Future of Europe

Hannah Hill

Table of contents

INTRODUCTION

The Rise of Viktor Orbán: From Liberal to Nationalist

Hungary's current prime minister, Viktor Mihály Orbán, has had an incredible political career.

Childhood and the Dissident Movement:
Orbán, who was born in Székesfehérvár, Hungary, on May 31, 1963, attended Eötvös Loránd University to study law.
He headed the Hungarian dissident student movement during the Revolutions of 1989, which marked the beginning of his political career.

He won national prominence in 1989 when he fearlessly asked that the Soviet military withdraw from Hungary in a speech that was crucial.

1998–2002, the first term as prime minister:
During his first term, Orbán accomplished a number of noteworthy goals, such as lowering the budget deficit, decreasing inflation, and getting Hungary into NATO.

His conservative coalition administration prioritized stability and economic improvements under his leadership.

From 2002 until 2010, the Opposition Leader:
Orbán was elected Leader of the Opposition in 2002 after his defeat in that election.
He refined his political maneuvers and established the foundation for his comeback to power during this time.

Current Second Premiership (2010 –):
2010 saw Orbán returned to the prime ministership, which he has maintained ever since.
Controversial constitutional amendments, legislative adjustments, and reactions to emergencies such as the COVID-19 epidemic and the European refugee crisis have characterized his second tenure.

Change in Ideology:
According to political analyst Zoltan Lakner, Orbán changed his views in the latter part of the 1990s.

Orbán understood that in order to win politically, he had to give up liberalism and turn his party into a nationalist, anti-liberal force, as Hungary was ruled by a liberal-socialist coalition.

Viktor Orbán's transition from a liberal upbringing to nationalist leadership illustrates the complexity of Hungary's political environment and his capacity for flexibility.

CHAPTER 1

THE EUROPEAN MIGRANT CRISIS: A PERFECT STORM

A powerful combination of conflict, hopelessness, and despair drove a record-breaking 1.2 million migrants and refugees toward the borders of Europe in 2015. Humanitarian disasters were caused by the Syrian Civil War, which was stoked by sectarian and geopolitical conflicts. Meanwhile, the unrest was exacerbated by the fall of Libya and the instability of Afghanistan.

The EU's unity and principles were tested when the migrant tsunami slammed against Europe's frontiers. Once a testament to transparency and collaboration, the Schengen Agreement started to deteriorate. Fences went up, borders shut, and the EU's core values of solidarity and freedom were strained to the limit.

Hungary became the center of the problem due to its advantageous location at the southeastern entrance of the EU. Already inclined toward nationalist and anti-immigrant discourse, Orbán's administration took advantage of the occasion to further its agenda. By skillfully combining rhetoric and political maneuvering, Orbán turned Hungary into a stronghold of opposition to the "migrant tide."

But there was a more intricate drama going on behind the scenes. EU leaders found it difficult to balance their humanitarian responsibilities with the political reality of a public that was becoming more and more doubtful. Once praised as a champion of immigrant rights, Angela Merkel of Germany now finds herself at conflict with her own supporters. As everything was going on, the EU's external frontiers turned into a battlefield, with Turkey and Libya emerging as major contenders in the chess match involving migrants.

As the crisis worsened, Orbán's Hungary turned into a far-right testing ground for measures that would fundamentally alter the political landscape of Europe. Everyone was wondering whether the European Union would become stronger and more cohesive or if the migrant crisis would signal the beginning of the end for the European ideal.

CHAPTER 3

THE HUNGARIAN MODEL: A BLUEPRINT FOR BORDER CONTROL

When refugees began pouring into Europe in the summer of 2015, Viktor Orbán's administration took immediate action. Hungary quickly and effectively built a strong wall around its southern border, surprising the EU.

The "Hungarian Model"—a framework for border management that would serve as a rallying cry for the far-right across Europe—was created.

The main parts of the model are:
- A new border police unit with the authority to drive out migrants and refugees;

-A 175-kilometer barrier strengthened with razor wire and monitoring technology.

-A system of detention facilities where people seeking refuge were housed in appalling circumstances.

-A legislative framework that deprives asylum applicants of their rights and criminalizes unlawful border crossing

Orbán's message was quite clear: the flood of migrants will not overrun Hungary. The EU found it difficult to react, having been taken aback by the former member state's unexpected aggressiveness. The EU's unity and principles came under pressure when far-right European politicians adopted the Hungarian Model.

CHAPTER 4

THE FENCE: A PHYSICAL BARRIER TO IMMIGRATION

The fence, an almost impassable wall, came to represent Hungary's strict immigration policies. Built in record speed, the fence became a formidable barrier for refugees and migrants across the southern border.

However, the fence served as more than a physical divide. It was a statement of national sovereignty, a philosophical divergence, and a rejection of the EU's open-border policy. Orbán made it very clear that Hungary would no longer accept migrants as a transit nation and that its borders would be guarded at all costs.

The dispute grew along with the barrier. Human rights organizations denounced the barrier as being against international law, and EU officials found it difficult to square Hungary's unilateral move with their own policy. The barrier evolved into a potent representation of the EU's immigration dilemma and a tangible representation of the

conflicts and divides that threatened to topple
the union.

CHAPTER 5

CRACKDOWN ON NGOS: THE 'STOP SOROS' LAWS

Orbán's administration focused on the non-governmental organizations (NGOs) that had been crucial in assisting refugees and migrants as the migration crisis worsened. The government began cracking down on these groups, claiming they were aiding illegal immigration and threatening Hungary's sovereignty.

The billionaire philanthropist George Soros was the inspiration for the "Stop Soros" regulations, which went after NGOs that supported migrant rights and took in foreign financing. Many were forced to close their doors or leave the nation as a result of the regulations' severe limitations on their activities.

The international world, the EU, and human rights organizations all strongly denounced the crackdown. Critics see it as an obvious effort to stifle opposing opinions and block humanitarian help. Unfazed, Orbán's administration maintained that the legislation was required to safeguard Hungary's cultural identity and national security.

The "Stop Soros" measures brought Hungary's ties with the EU to a new low and raised questions about the deterioration of democratic principles and the rule of law. Hungarian democracy was at risk as the impasse between Budapest and Brussels became more intense.

CHAPTER 6

MIGRANT LIVES MATTER: THE HUMAN COST OF ORBÁN'S POLICIES

Orbán's actions have had an absolutely disastrous effect on migrants and asylum seekers. The actions taken have caused great misery for people; many lives have been lost, families have been shattered, and hope has been lost.

The increase in migrant fatalities has been one of the most terrible effects. Although the dangerous trek to Europe has always been risky, Orbán's measures have increased the danger. As a result of being compelled to travel dangerous routes to avoid being discovered by police, the number of deaths rises. Thousands of migrants have died trying to reach the coasts of Europe, turning the Mediterranean Sea into a cemetery.

Those that make it through the trek are treated cruelly and with hatred. Hungary's detention camps have been compared as "prison-like" establishments, where refugees endure filthy surroundings, extreme congestion, and limited access to basic amenities like food, water, and healthcare. There have been reports of migrants being abused physically and psychologically by officials, leaving them defenseless and traumatized.

In addition, family separations brought about by Orbán's policies have left children abandoned and alone. These young people have experienced unimaginable tragedy, which will have a lasting impact on them for years to come. Women have been disproportionately impacted, experiencing marginalization, discrimination, and violence based on their gender.

One cannot emphasize how detrimental Orbán's policies are to mental health. Many migrants have attempted suicide or self-harm after being driven to the verge of hopelessness. Their sense of self-worth has been damaged by their inability to access fundamental human rights like respect and dignity, which has left them feeling forlorn and powerless.

Syrian Amir, 25, left Aleppo after learning that a blast had murdered his family. With little more than hope and crumbs, he made his way across Greece and Turkey. He was arrested and assaulted by police when he arrived in Hungary.

With memories haunting his eyes, Amir remarked, "I just wanted safety." "But they treated me like a criminal."

The 30-year-old Afghan woman Fatima and her two kids managed to flee the violence of the Taliban. After trekking over rivers and mountains, Hungarian police forced them to retreat.

"I saw my children shivering in the cold," Fatima wept. "I felt like I failed them."

Twenty-year-old Somali Mohammed was held in a Hungarian prison facility for eighteen months. Without any paperwork, a phone, or any hope, he was let free.

"I feel like a ghost," Mohammed said, his voice barely audible. "Invisible and forgotten."

These stories are a testament to the human cost of Orbán's policies. They serve as a reminder that immigrants and refugees are people with rights to justice, compassion, and dignity—not simply numbers or political pawns.

Orbán's actions have had a disastrous human cost. The compassion and dignity of migrant lives have been overlooked, turning them into nothing more than numbers. It is critical that we never forget that immigrant lives count and that they should be treated with respect, compassion, and safety while the world looks on. The results of Orbán's actions serve as a sobering warning about the perils of racism, xenophobia, and the dehumanization of immigrants. To make sure that their lives are respected and safeguarded, we must respond quickly and empathetically.

CHAPTER 7

HUMAN RIGHTS CONCERNS: CRITICISM FROM THE EU AND INTERNATIONAL COMMUNITY

The European Union and the world community have strongly criticized the policies and actions of the Hungarian government, raising serious concerns about abuses of human rights. Human rights groups, the EU, and specialists have denounced Hungary's harsh and antithetical handling of migrants, refugees, and asylum seekers.

The incarceration of migrants and asylum seekers in border camps, sometimes in filthy circumstances, is one of the most divisive topics. Alarming reports of excessive force by authorities, poor access to food, water, and medical treatment, and overcrowding have been made public. Hungary's government has refused to budge despite repeated requests from the EU for it to solve these issues.

The limitations placed on the rights of asylum seekers are another matter of concern. Laws that restrict asylum applicants' capacity to challenge denied claims have been implemented in Hungary, making them more susceptible to deportation. The EU's regulation on asylum processes and international law pertaining to refugees have both been cited as being broken by this action.

Concern regarding Hungary's treatment of vulnerable populations, such as women, children, and LGBTQ+ people, has also been voiced by the international community. The Hungarian government has been urged to intervene after reports of marginalization, discrimination, and violence against women have emerged.

Hungary has been under constant EU pressure to uphold the rule of law and respect for human rights, with threats of fines if reforms are not implemented. International human rights groups have also denounced Hungary's conduct and demanded a halt to the abuse of refugees and asylum seekers, including Human Rights Watch and Amnesty International.

The EU and the international community have expressed serious concerns about the government's policies and actions, putting Hungary's human rights record under rigorous scrutiny. It is unclear whether Hungary will address these issues and honor its obligations to the rule of law and human rights as the crisis develops.

CHAPTER 8

THE ECONOMIC IMPACT: DOES ORBÁN'S POLICY PAY OFF?

Supporters of Orbán have hailed his initiatives as a great success, but the data on the economy reveals a more complex picture. Hungary's economy has expanded, but Orbán's initiatives have come at a high cost and the advantages have mostly benefited a small number of people.

The brain drain has been one of the biggest financial losses. The smartest and most talented people in Hungary have been fleeing the nation in large numbers in search of opportunities inside the EU. Hungary has lost the knowledge and experience necessary to spur innovation and expansion as a result of this talent flight.

Foreign investment has also significantly decreased as a result of Orbán's policies. Hungary's unfriendly economic climate, which is marked by arbitrary rules, corruption, and a lack of transparency, has discouraged multinational firms. Foreign direct investment, which has traditionally been a major factor in Hungary's economic development, has significantly decreased as a consequence of this.

In addition, there have been significant expenditures for the construction and upkeep of the border barrier in addition to the price of processing and holding migrants. The Hungarian taxpayer is bearing a heavy weight as a result of these expenses, with estimates indicating that the cost of the border barrier alone may surpass €1 billion.

Hungary's economy has grown in spite of these expenses, mostly due to EU financing and a positive global economic climate. Nevertheless, there hasn't been much of a trickle-down effect to the general populace; instead, this expansion has been mostly focused among the rich few. Numerous Hungarians are still struggling to make ends meet, and poverty and inequality continue to be serious problems.

There have been some economic gains from Orbán's policies, but they have come at a high cost and have mostly benefited a small group of people. Hungary's economy has suffered as a result of the brain drain, a drop in foreign investment, and high costs related to the border barrier and migrant detention. The nation must carefully weigh the economic effects of its decisions going ahead and work to develop a more sustainable and inclusive economic model that serves all Hungarians.

CHAPTER 9

PARALLELS BETWEEN ORBÁN'S HUNGARY AND TRUMP'S AMERICA

The United States should take note from the emergence of authoritarianism in Hungary under Viktor Orbán's leadership. There are a lot of interesting similarities between Orbán's Hungary and Trump's America, which need further thought.

First off, in order to maintain control, both leaders have taken advantage of worries and concerns around immigration and national security. Trump's own immigration policies, such as the divisive travel ban aimed at mostly Muslim nations, are a reflection of Orbán's anti-immigrant rhetoric and actions.

Second, press freedom has been threatened by both leaders' attacks on the media. In order to quiet dissenting opinions, Orbán's administration has used intimidation and litigation, while Trump has often referred to the media as "enemies of the people" and "fake news."

Thirdly, the rule of law and institutional independence have been compromised by both leaders. Orbán's administration has stacked the election commission and courts with supporters, while Trump has consistently criticized the legal system and demanded political allegiance from the Justice Department.

Fourth, in order to energize their supporters and foster a "us versus them" mindset, both leaders have used divisive language. While Trump has attacked immigrants, minorities, and the political establishment, Orbán has blamed immigration and the EU for Hungary's woes.

Last but not least, both leaders have shown a disdain for the truth and the facts. Trump has been charged with lying and promoting conspiracy theories, while Orbán's administration has disseminated propaganda and false information.

The striking similarities between Orbán's Hungary and Trump's America serve as a timely reminder of how precarious democracy is and how vigilant it must be at all times.

Hungary's decline in democratic institutions and values should serve as a cautionary tale for the US, emphasizing how crucial it is to defend press freedom, the rule of law, and institutional autonomy. America has to take a cue from Hungary as it navigates its own political issues and reject authoritarian impulses that pose a danger to its democratic roots.

CHAPTER 10

LESSONS LEARNED: WHAT THE US CAN TAKE AWAY FROM HUNGARY'S EXPERIENCE

The United States can learn a lot from Hungary's slide toward totalitarianism under Viktor Orbán's direction. Hungary's history offers valuable lessons for America as it faces its own political difficulties.

First and foremost, it is crucial to safeguard democratic institutions. There have been disastrous ramifications from Hungary's deterioration of journalistic freedom, election integrity, and judicial independence.
The US has to make sure its institutions are strong and autonomous.

Second, there is no doubt about the risks associated with using scapegoating and divisive language.
The political atmosphere has become poisonous due to Orbán's anti-EU and anti-migrant rhetoric. The US ought to

discourage such strategies and encourage inclusive, fact-based dialogue.

Thirdly, it is imperative that civil society has a role in holding leaders responsible. Journalists, NGOs, and activists from Hungary have bravely opposed Orbán's government. To guarantee that democratic norms are maintained, the US must strengthen and assist its own civil society.

Fourth, there's a warning that the EU is doing little to stop Hungary's retreat. In its foreign policy, the US should place a high priority on democracy and human rights and assist international organizations that uphold these principles.

Last but not least, the tenacity of Hungarian democracy proves that hope for rebirth exists even in the worst of circumstances. The US should take a cue from Hungary and strive for a more promising future for all.

Ultimately, the tale of Hungary is a potent reminder of the need of defending democracy, advocating for inclusive language, assisting civil society, giving human rights first priority in foreign policy, and maintaining vigilance in the face of tyranny. These are lessons that the US has to keep in mind as it negotiates its own political terrain in order to guarantee that its democracy endures for many decades to come.

CHAPTER 11

WARNING SIGNS: THE EROSION OF DEMOCRATIC Norms And Rise Of Nationalism

There are notable parallels between Hungary and the US in the growth of nationalism and the deterioration of democratic standards. Minority rights have been suppressed, political debate has declined, and institutions have become more politicized in both nations.

Indicators of concern in the US include:

1. Political polarization: As differences and intolerance have grown, polite conversation has decreased and common ground has been lost.

2. Assaults on the media: Frequent assaults on the media and the designation of negative reporting as "fake news" impair the ability of a free press to hold public officials responsible.

3. Erosion of public faith in institutions: The public's trust has decreased as a result of ongoing assaults on the electoral system, the judiciary, and other institutions.

4. Rise of nationalist discourse: The rhetoric that is dividing the country, emphasizing "America First" and anti-immigrant feeling, is reminiscent of Hungary.

5. Suppression of minority rights: Marginalized populations are disproportionately affected by attempts to curtail voting rights, gerrymander districts, and restrict access to social services and healthcare.

These indicators point to a risky trend toward authoritarianism that is similar to Hungary's. To stop the further deterioration of democratic standards and save its democratic underpinnings, the US has to acknowledge and confront these developments.

The US may take proactive measures to improve its democracy, encourage inclusive language, and make sure that the rise of nationalism does not come at the expense of democratic principles by taking note of

Hungary's experience and recognizing the warning signals at home.

CONCLUSION

The Future of Immigration Policy: A Call to Action

A sobering reminder of the significance of upholding democratic norms and encouraging welcoming immigration policies is provided by the tale of Hungary's decline into authoritarianism and the emergence of nationalism in the US. It is obvious that the decisions we make today will influence the path of history for future generations as we look to the future.

The United States of America has a rare chance to take a different approach and learn from Hungary's mistakes. The US can make sure that its democracy is robust and resilient by putting a high priority on democratic values, encouraging fact-based debate, and supporting inclusive immigration policies.

Building blocks for future immigration policy should be the following:

1. **Empathy**: Honor the humanity and dignity of each and every immigrant and refugee.

2. **Facts**: Rely on data and facts when making policy judgments rather than hunches and false information.

3. **Inclusion**: Create laws that encourage fusion and deal with the underlying reasons for migration.

4.Work together with international partners to confront the world's refugee problem and advance sustainable development.

5. **Democracy**: Make certain that democratic principles and the rule of law inform immigration policy.

It's obvious what has to be done. Collaboratively, let us construct a future that upholds the principles of democracy, empathy, and diversity. Instead of pursuing a course that fosters separation and fear, let's reject politics and embrace a more optimistic future for everybody.

The direction of immigration policy is a moral need as well as a technical one. Taking on this task, let's create a more equitable, caring, and democratic society for all.

APPENDIX

Timeline of Key Events:

A chronological list of major events related to Orbán's rise to power and anti-immigration policies

- Hungary's first prime minister, Viktor Orbán, took office in 1998 and remained in that position until 2002.

- 2002
After his party, Fidesz, loses the election, Orbán becomes the leader of the opposition.

-2010
With a resounding triumph, Fidesz takes the prime ministership, and Orbán returns.

- 2015
Hundreds of thousands of migrants arrive in Europe, marking the height of the migration crisis in Europe.

- 2015
A border barrier being erected by Orbán's administration along the Serbian border.

- 2016

A legislation enabling the automatic detention of all asylum seekers is passed by Orbán's administration.

- 2017

Hungary's detention of asylum seekers is declared unlawful by the European Court of Justice.

-2018

A legislation making it illegal to aid illegal immigration is passed by Orbán's administration.

- 2019

The European Parliament decides to penalize Hungary under Article 7 for violating EU principles.

-2020

Legislation enabling the government to rule by decree during the COVID-19 pandemic was passed by Orbán's administration.

Hungary enacts a legislation in 2021 prohibiting the dissemination of materials that encourage gender identity or homosexuality in schools.

– 2022
A legislation authorizing the building of a new border barrier along the Ukrainian border is passed by Orbán's administration.

– Hungary enacts legislation in **2023** that limits asylum applicants' capacity to challenge denials of claims.

– 2024
The government of Viktor Orbán declares that a nationwide vote on EU immigration policy will be held.

– January 2024
Citing worries about rule of law and corruption, the European Commission opens a probe into Hungary's use of EU money.

–March 2024
A legislation limiting asylum seekers' access to healthcare and education was passed by Orbán's administration.

– May 2024

Hungary's limitations on asylum seekers' access to healthcare and education are declared unlawful by the European Court of Justice.

GLOSSARY OF TERMS

Asylum Seeker: An individual who has left their home country due to a well-founded fear of persecution, war, or natural disaster and is seeking protection in another country.

Article 7: A provision in the Treaty on European Union that allows the EU to suspend or remove a member state's voting rights if it breaches EU values.

Border Fence: A physical barrier constructed along a country's border to prevent illegal crossings.

EU Values: The fundamental principles and values that underpin the European Union, including democracy, the rule of law, and human rights.

Fidesz: The political party led by Viktor Orbán, which has been the ruling party in Hungary since 2010.

Illegal Immigration: The act of entering a country without proper documentation or authorization.

Migration Policy: The rules and regulations governing the entry and stay of foreign nationals in a country.

Refugee: An individual who has been granted protection in another country due to a well-founded fear of persecution, war, or natural disaster.

Rule of Law: The principle that all individuals, institutions, and government officials are subject to the law and must act in accordance with it.

Sanctions: Measures imposed by the EU on a member state that breaches EU values or rules, such as suspending voting rights or withholding funding.

Schengen Area: A group of EU countries that have abolished border controls and allow free movement of citizens between them.

Visegrád Group: A regional alliance of four Central European countries (Hungary, Poland,

Czech Republic, and Slovakia) that coordinates their policies on migration, security, and other issues.

About the author

Hannah Hill is a seasoned political analyst and writer with over 10 years of experience, specializing in international affairs, migration policy, and global trends. With a keen eye for detail and a passion for storytelling, she provides insightful analysis on the complex issues shaping our world, from the United States to Europe and beyond. Her expertise has been honed through a decade of researching, writing, and commenting on global political developments, making her a trusted voice in the field.